Enjoy the walk/s and may I wish you Happy Walking!

"May your boots feel as comy as slippers,
Your rucksack as light as a feather.
May the sun shine all day and the wind
by at your back.
May you go in peace,
with joy in your heart,
and enjoy being reconnected to Mother Earth."

Happy walking!
Revd. John N. Merrill

Shinrin-Yoku
- The healing art of Japanese Forest bathing.

I have quite naturally, been doing this all my life on my walks. By simply going for a walk, on my own, brings huge benefits, not just breathing in clean fresh air but getting exercise and connecting with the sacred world around us. We are connected to and one with everything. The only way to appreciate and deeply understand nature and all its beauty and wonder is by being alone.....quite simply miracles occur.

Walk peacefully through a wood and just observe the leaves, the berries, the way a tree grows, the flowers that carpet the floor. Stop, sit and listen to the bird song, or watch a squirrel rooting among the leaves. By being still and observant many other animals and features come into view. Sit at the base of tree and feel its strength and wisdom. Sit by a tinkling stream and observe the wildlife that inhabits this domain. Lie on the ground and gaze at the sky and watch the clouds pass over, or at night the whole cosmos becomes visible. Find an old oak tree and give it a hug. Communicate with the birds, they will sing back to you and hop onto other branches to get a clearer view. Talk to the flowers, caress their leaves and admire their delicate design and smell their fragrance. If you feel hungry eat some wild blackberries. The natural world has much to teach us and enlivens our soul getting back to the basics of life. Return home refreshed and invigorated and go about your day with more vigour, purpose and energy. Then after a few days go back again and rejuvenate your being.

www.shinrin-yoku.org
(Revd. John N. Merrill - February 2019).

John Merrill's Surrey Hills Challenge Walk
by Revd. John N. Merrill

The Day Challenge Walk Series - Vol. 33
THE JOHN MERRILL FOUNDATION

JOHN MERRILL WALK GUIDES
32, HOLMESDALE, WALTHAM CROSS,
HERTFORDSHIRE. EN8 8QY

Tel/ Fax 01992 762776
Email - marathonhiker@aol.com

www.johnmerrillwalkguides.co.uk
www.thejohnmerrillministry.co.uk

International Copyright - John Merrill. All rights reserved. No part of this publication may be reproduced or transmitted in any form or by any means electronic or mechanical including photocopy, recording or any information storage or retrieval system in any place, in any country without the prior permission of The John Merrill Foundation.

Revd. John N. Merrill asserts his moral rights to be identified as the author of this work.

A catalogue record for this book is available from the British Library,

Conceived, edited, typset and designed by The John Merrill Foundation.
Printed and handmade by Revd. John N. Merrill.
Book layout and cover design by Revd. John N. Merrill.

Copyright - Text and photographs - Revd. John N. Merrill 2014.
Copyright - Map - Revd. John N. Merrill 2014.

ISBN 978-0-9927816-8-2

First Published - November 2014.   Special limited edition.
Cover picture - by Revd. John N. Merrill.

Typeset in Aharoni - bold, italic and plain 11pt, 14pt and 18pt.

John Merrill confirms he has walked all the routes in this book and detailed what he found at the time of walking. The publishers, however cannot be held responsible for alterations, errors, omissions, or for changes in details given. They would welcome information to help keep the book upto date.

The John Merrill Foundation maintains the John Merrill Library and archives and administers the worldwide publishing rights of John Merrill's works in all media formats.

The John Merrill Foundation plants sufficient trees through the Woodland Trust to replenish the trees used in its publications.

A little about Revd. John N. Merrill

June 2019 walking the English Camino to Santiago de Compostela.

John is unique, possessing the skills of a marathon runner, mountain climber and athlete. Since his first 1,000 mile walk through the islands of the Inner and Outer Hebrides in 1970, he has since walked over 220,500 miles and worn out 136 pairs of boots, 49 rucksacks and more than 1,600 pairs of socks. He has brought marathon walking to Olympic standard. He has done a 1,000 mile walk through the Orkneys and Shetlands and a 1,600 mile walk up the whole length of the west coast of Ireland. In 1978 he became the first person to walk around the entire coastline of Britain - 7,000 miles - and at the same completed a 4,300 mile Land's End to John O'Groats walks and climbing the three peaks on the way 1,814 miles. He has walked across Europe, the Alps and Pyrenees - 3,000 miles with 600,000 feet of ascent and descent. In America he has walked the 2,500 mile Appalachian Trail; the Pacific Crest Trail - 2,500 miles in record time; the Continental Divide Trail; became the first person to thru-hike the Buckeye Trail - 1,350 miles in Ohio and completed a unique 4,260 mile walk in 178 days coast to coast across America. He has climbed all the mountains in New Mexico and walked all the trails.

In Britain he has walked all the National Trails many times; linked all the National Parks and trails in a 2,060 mile walk; completed a 1,608 mile Land's End to John o' Groats walk and countless other unique walks including 450 miles from Norwich to Durham Cathedral. He has walked four times to Santiago de Compostella (Spain) via different routes - 2,800 miles, and from Paris, Arles and Holland.; to St. Olav's Shrine in Norway - 420 miles; walked to Assisi, St. Gilles du Gard, three Cathar Ways and to Mont St. Michel, three times, including one by bicycle from Paris to Mont St. Michel & St. Malo - 340 miles in 2018. He has walked every long distance path in France and Germany, and to every pilgrimage destination in England, France and Europe, and extensively walked and skied in every country in Europe, America, Canada and India.

He has walked in Africa; all the trails in the Hong Kong Islands; and completed five trekking expeditions to the Himalayas and India. Not only is he the world's leading marathon walker he is Britain's most experienced walker. John is author of more than 460 walk guides which have sold more than 4 million copies with more than 1 million sold on the Peak District alone. He has created more than 80 challenge walks which have been used to raise, so far, more than a £1.2 million for different charities.

John has never broken a bone or been lost and never had any trouble anywhere. He still walks in the same body he was born with, has had no replacements and does not use walking poles. This he puts down to his deep spiritual nature and in 2010 he was ordained as a multi-faith Minister - a universal monk, *"honouring and embracing all faiths and none"*. He conducts many Wedding Services - one in Sarajevo, Bosnia and so far, more than 500 Funeral services; he teaches Qigong and is a Reiki practioner. He gives talks all over the UK.

Abinger Hammer Clock - "By me you know how fast to go".

CONTENTS

Page No.

About John N. Merrill 3
Introduction 7
How to do it 8
About the Walk 9
How to do a walk 10
The Art of Walking the John Merrill Way 11

THE WALK -

Abinger Hammer to Wotton - 3 miles 12
Wotton to Colldharbour - 4 miles 16
Coldharbour to Holmbury St. Mary - 4 miles 20
Holmbury St. Mary to Ewhurst Windmill - 5 miles 24
Ewhurst Windmill to Shere - 5 miles 30
Shere to Abinger Hammer - 2 miles 34

Observe the Country Code 37
Walk Log 38
Badge & Certificate Order Form 39
Other books by Revd. John N. Merrill 40

View of the North Downs from the path near Wotton.

INTRODUCTION

My final preparations for walking around the entire coastline of Britain, was the Pilgrim' Way from Winchester to Canterbury; reaching there on Christmas eve. The walk was fascinating with many remarkable places and historical buildings. One place that stood out was Abinger Hammer, and although a small village it made an impression.

Many years later I have twice walked from the Thames at Kingston on Thames, following the Down Link path to the North Downs Way near Box Hill. The route doesn't go to the summit, but I always do, for the view and completeness. On my last walk a month ago I realised that I had not walked the North Downs Way in its entirety, although I have walked many sections of it over the years. Standing on Box Hill, I resolved to correct this oversight and the next week was in Farnham and walking the way. I eventually came above Gomsall and knew it was another three hours walking to Dorking, so I descended to Gomsall. Here I learnt I had missed the train and the next was in 2 hours time! I should have carried on to Dorking!

But, there was a meaning to all this. A few days later I was back in Dorking and caught the bus to Abinger Hammer, close to Gomsall, and I could retrace my steps back onto the way and walk onto to Dorking and Mertsham. It was while I was on St. Martha's Hill the first day and looked at the view to Leith Hill, arguably the highest point in S.E. England, that I realised I had not explored the Surrey Hills.

Back at my desk, later, I looked at the maps and "saw" a circular walk from Abinger Hammer over the Surrey high spots to Leith Hill and back via the stunning village of Shere. I interrupted my walk along the North Downs, and two days later was back in Abinger Hammer and set off on this walk! It was all meant to be.

The sun shone and as always I did no research, just worked out a natural linking route around the area. That's the beauty of not knowing what is just around the corner until you get there. I came and discovered many interesting places, saw a wide variety of birds, and numerous impressive trees, now tinged with autumn colours. But, it is the views I remember most; Leith Hill has an extraordinary panorama, but several other hills provided stunning views. I took little over 8 hours to do the walk and was sad it was over. I'm glad the bus only went to Abinger Hammer and reacquainted myself with this choice piece of scenery and history.

I hope the suns shines for you all day; the views unfold in all their majesty; the trees sway in the gentle breeze; the birds sing and the squirrels scamper nonchalantly away up a tree as you pass. Enjoy the walk.

Happy walking!   John N. Merrill   October 2014.

HOW TO DO IT

The whole walk is covered by the following O.S. 1:25,000 **Explorer maps Nos.** -

- *No. 145 – Guildford & Farnham.*
- *No, 146 – Dorking, Box Hill & Reigate.*

The circular challenge walk is designed to be done in about 8 to 9 hours. The route follows well defined path/tracks and takes you over the highest hills in Surrey and S.E. England. So choose a fine day to make the most of the extensive views.

There are several inns along the way but little else. The village of Shere, near the end, has shops. Be self contained and basically carry what you need for the day. There is a tea-room in Abinger Hammer.

There is a small Village parking in Abinger Hammer, at the start of the road to Holmbury St. Mary, on the left and where the bus stops from Dorking. The village is on the regular bus routes from Dorking and Guildford and Holmbury St. Mary – close to halfway – also has a more limited bus service to Dorking; there is a Youth Hostel here, unfortunately well off the route!

The John Merrill Foundation maintains a register of successful walkers and a badge and certificate are available from them - see order form at the rear of the book.

Apt words on a van at the start of the walk in Hackhurst Lane.

ABOUT THE WALK

Whilst every care is taken detailing and describing the walk in this book, it should be borne in mind that the countryside changes by the seasons and the work of man. I have described the walk to the best of my ability, detailing what I have found actually on the walk in the way of stiles and signs. You should always walk with the appropriate O.S. map, as detailed for each walk, open on the walk area for constant reference. Obviously with the passage of time stiles become broken or replaced by a ladder stile , a small gate or a kissing gate. Signs too have a habit of being broken or pushed over - vandalism. All the route follow rights of way and only on rare occasions will you have to overcome obstacles in its path, such as a blown down tree, barbed wire fence or an electric fence. On rare occasions rights of way are rerouted and these amendments are included in the next edition. Inns have a frustrating habit of changing their name, then back to the original one!

All rights of way have colour coded arrows; on marker posts, stiles/gates and trees; these help you to show the direction of the right of way -

>Yellow - Public footpath.
>Blue - Public bridleway.
>Red - Byway open to all traffic (BOAT).
>Black - Road used as a public path (RUPP).
>White - Concessionary and Permissive path

The seasons bring occasional problems whilst out walking which should also be borne in mind. In the height of summer paths become overgrown and you may have to fight your way through in a few places. In low lying areas the fields are often full of crops, and although the pathline goes straight across it may be more practical to walk round the field edge to get to the next stile or gate. In summer the ground is generally dry but in autumn and winter, especially because of our climate, the surface can be decidedly wet and slippery; sometimes even gluttonous mud!

These comments are part of countryside walking which help to make your walk more interesting or briefly frustrating. Standing in a track up to your ankles in mud might not be funny at the time but upon reflection was one of the highlights of the walk!

The mileage for each section is based on three calculations -

1. pedometer and stepometer readings.
2. the route map measured on the map.
3. the time I took for the walk.

I believe the figure stated for each section to be very accurate but we all walk differently and not always in a straight line! The time allowed for each section is on the generous side and does not include pub stops etc. The figure is based on the fact that on average a person walks 2 1/2 miles an hours but less in hilly terrain. Allow 20 minutes to walk a mile; ten minutes for 1/2 mile and five minutes for 1/4 mile. On average you will walk 2,000 strides to a mile - an average stride is 31 inches..

HOW TO DO A WALK

The walks in this book follow public right of ways, be it a footpath, bridleway, BOAT or RUPP, which are marked on the Ordnance Survey 1:25,000 Explorer Series of maps.

On each walk I have detailed which maps are needed and I would urge you to carry and use a map. As I walk I always have the map out on the section I am walking, constantly checking that I am walking the right way. Also when coming to any road or path junction, I can check on the map to ensure I take the right route.

Most paths are signed and waymarked with coloured arrows - yellow for footpaths; blue for bridleways - but I would at best describe them as intermittent. They act as confirmation of the right of way you are walking and the arrow usually point in the direction of travel.

The countryside has the added problem of vandalism and you will find path logo's and Information Boards spray painted over and even path signs pointing the wrong way! That is why I always advise carrying the map open on the area you are walking to check you are walking the right way. In my walking instructions I have given the name and number of each main and minor road, canal lock and bridge number, together with house numbers where you turn and the name of the inns passed. Wherever I add what the footpath sign says, plus the stiles, footbridges and kissing gates en route. All to help you have a smooth and trouble free walk.

I confirm that I have walked every route and written what I found at the time of walking.

Most people don't walk correctly with a straight spine and feet parallel to each other, and a few inches apart. Each step starts the cycle of lifting the foot a little way off the ground and placing the heel down first, then moving forward as the foot bends with the toes being last to leave the ground as the cycle begins again. It is all a gentle fluid rolling motion; with practice you can glide across the terrain, effortlessly, for mile after mile.

THE ART OF WALKING
THE JOHN MERRILL WAY

1. **Always set off in the clothes you plan to wear all day**, given the weather conditions. Only on sudden changes in the weather will I stop and put on a waterproof or warmer clothing.

2. **Set off at a steady comfortable pace**, which you can maintain all day. You should end the walk as fresh as when as you started.

3. **Maintain your pace and don't stop.** Stopping for any period of time disrupts your rhythm and takes upwards of a mile to settle back down into the flow/ease of movement.

4. **Switch off your mobile phone and music centre**, and listen and enjoy the countryside - the smells of the flowers, bird song, the rustle of the leaves and the tinkling stream.

5. **Ignore the mileage and ascents** - don't tick off the miles, just concentrate on what the walk's goal is. To think otherwise slows you down and makes the walk a struggle rather than a joy. In a similar vein, when ascending just keep a steady pace and keep going. To stop is to disrupt the flow and make the ascent interminable.

6. **Whilst a walk is a challenge to complete, it is not just exercise.** You should enjoy the world around you; the flowers, birds, wildlife and nature and look at and explore the historical buildings and church's that you pass. All are part of life's rich tapestry.

7. **Remember that for every mile that you walk, you extend your life by** 21 **minutes.**

8. **A journey of a** 1,000 **miles begins with a single step and a mile requires** 2,000 **strides.**

"The journey begins when you close the door behind you" JNM

"The expert traveller leaves no footprints." Lao Tzu.

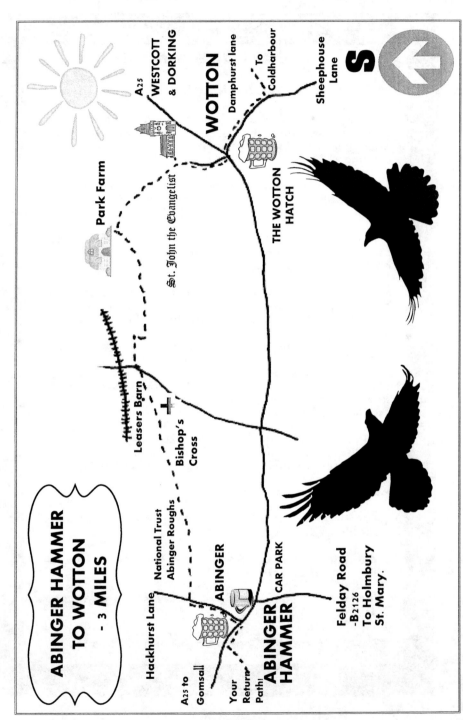

ABINGER HAMMER TO WOTTON
– 3 MILES
– allow 1 hour.

Maps – OS 1:25,000 *Explorer Series Nos* -
- *145* – *Guildford & Farnham.*
- *146* – *Dorking, Box Hill & Reigate.*

Car parking – *Small Village parking are in Abinger Hammer, at the start of the road, on left, to Holmbury St. Mary – Felday Road – B2126.*

Inns – Abinger, Abinger Hammer. The Wotton Hatch, Wotton.

Tea Room – Abinger Hammer.

ABOUT THE SECTION – From the fascinating and unspoilt village of Abinger Hammer, you ascend into woodland to follow a well defined path/track. En route you have some stunning views of the North Downs. You pass a cross marking the spot where the Bishop of Winchester fell off his horse and died. At Park Farm you turn right and begin the "ascent" to Leith Hill. You pass St. John the Evangelist church of Wotton before reaching the A25 road opposite the Wotton Hatch Inn.

WALKING INSTRUCTIONS – Starting from Abinger Hammer on the A25, aim for the Abinger Hammer Clock and blacksmith bell ringer, with the Abinger inn just after. Before it turn right up Hackhurst Lane, opposite String Antiques. Ascend the sunken lane for ¼ mile to the open countryside and the Cycleway No. 22 that crosses the lane. Turn right onto cycleway, which is just a path, and enter the National Trust property – Abinger Roughs. Reach a gate and keep straight ahead, now along a track – still part of the cycleway. You reach a height of 138m and descend in woodland to a bridle-path sign. Keep straight ahead, now on the edge of the woodland on your right. Pass the cross marking the tragic spot of the Bishop of Winchester death, with Leasers Barn on the left. You pass many fine beech trees here. Soon after reach a lane and turn left and right, and still of the cycleway.

The views from here to the North Downs escarpment and to Box Hill are excellent. Follow the path by the wood's edge, soon turning right and then left as you walk through a large area of pine trees. Continue to Park Farm, now on a track, and follow it left to the house entrance and path sign. Turn half right and follow the path diagonally across and up the field to a kissing gate and woodland. Keep ahead on the now fenced path which in ¼ mile brings you to the end of the Church Lane with St. John the Evangelist church on your left. Follow the lane down and round to the left, passing the top of a shallow dale on your left, and reach the A25 road, opposite The Wotton Hatch inn. Cross and keep left along Damphurst Lane.

ABINGER HAMMER – The clock in memory of the first Lord Farrer of Abinger Hall, who died in 1899. "Jack the Blacksmith" strikes the bell every hour. The motto says - "By me you know how fast to go". The River Tillingbourne flows through a meadow and was harnassed in the 16th. Century to provide water power for Abinger Forge.

Path in Abinger Roughs - National Trust property.

14

BISHOP OF WINCHESTER – Samuel Wilberforce, the third son of the slave abolitionist, William Wilberforce, was a renowned public speaker. He was Bishop of Winchester 1870 – 1873. A colourful character who lived a full life, enjoying hunting and nude running in his youth. He fell off his horse, aged 67, on July 19th, 1873, and the shock killed him. The memorial cross marks the spot.

ST. JOHN THE EVANGELIST CHURCH – Has Saxon origins; the tower is Norman, but much work was carried out during the Victorian era. Inside is the Evelyn Chapel with several impressive monuments and the tomb of John Evelyn, the diarist. Members of the Vaughan Williams family are buried just to the right of the building.

WOTTON – Recorded in the Domesday Book as Odetone.

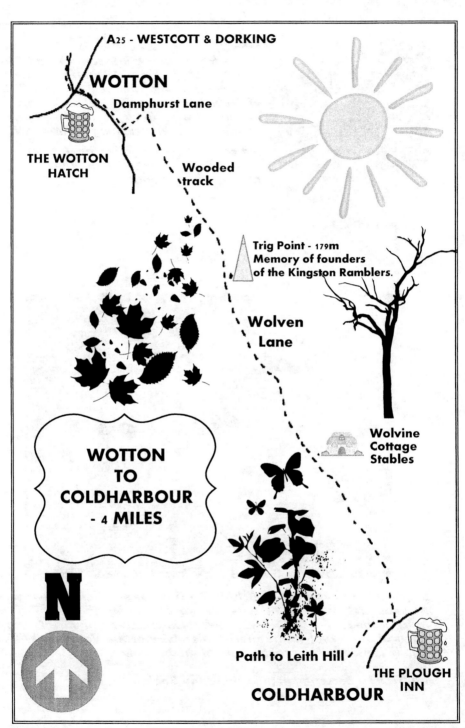

WOTTON to COLDHARBOUR
– 4 MILES
– allow 1 ½ hour.

Map – OS 1:25,000 Explorer Series No 146 – Dorking, Box Hill & Reigate

Inns – The Wotton Hatch, Wotton. The Plough Inn, Coldharbour.

ABOUT THE SECTION – All along a well defined track (Wolvens Lane) in woodland – mostly pine and beech. You are basically ascending, gently, most of the way from 137m to 250m a.s.l. – about 400 feet of ascent, which you don't really notice! After heavy rain the track can be full of large puddles, but most of the time there is a path on the right-hand side keeping to higher ground. Views unfold southwards at Coldharbour, with an inn and an Iron Age fort – Anstiebury to the left in trees.

WALKING INSTRUCTIONS – At the A25 in Wotton, opposite The Wotton Hatch, cross the road and bear left along Damphurst Lane. Pass houses on the right and the Surrey Hills Business Park on the left. Shortly after turn left onto a Public Byway and join the Greensands Way; at this junction the way goes left – our route and right to Leith Hill – you will meet up with this path later. For now keep left along the track – Greensands Way – to the next path junction. Here the Greensands Way turns left; we turn right onto the wooded track which is also a Public Byway – Wolvens Lane – which you follow straight ahead for more than 3 miles to the road at Coldharbour.

The track, sunken at first, passes through mature woodland with many fine beech and pine trees and swathes of silver birch. In almost a mile pass the Trig point 179m. which has a memorial plaque to the two founders of the Kingston Rambling Club. Continue straight ahead, ignoring all side paths and in another mile reach Wolvens Cottage Stables on the left. Keep ahead and in ¾ mile you descend and pass Cockers Farm Livery and gain the road in Coldharbour opposite The Plough Inn.

Wolvens Lane.

Pine woodland near Coldharbour.

Trig Point - 179m.
Kingston Rambling Club Memorial.

GREENSANDS WAY – *108 mile long path following the greensand ridge from Haselmere in Surrey to Hamstreet, Kent.*

COLDHARBOUR – *The highest village in southern England with a population of some 240 people.*

ANSTIEBURY – *Iron Age fort from the 1st and 2nd Centuries BC.*

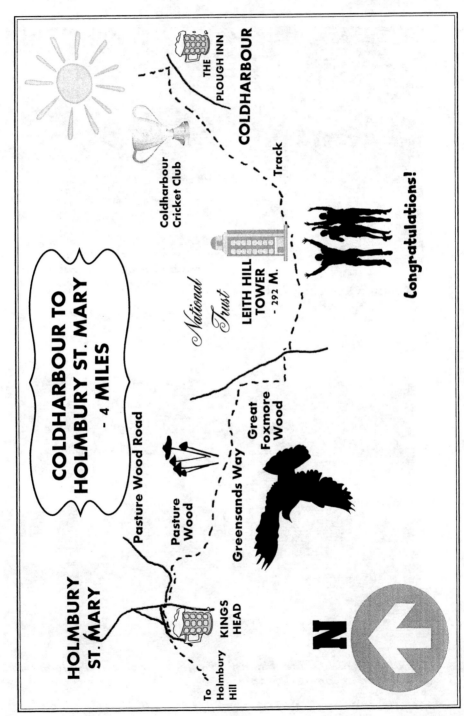

COLDHARBOUR to HOLMBURY ST. MARY – 4 MILES – allow 1 ½ hour.

Map – OS 1:25,000 Explorer Series No 146 – Dorking, Box Hill & Reigate.

Inns – The Plough Inn, Coldharbour. Kings Head, Holmbury St. Mary.

ABOUT THE SECTION – Your effort will soon be rewarded as you continue ascending and finally steeply to the tower on Leith Hill, the highest point in S.E. England-. The tower, owned by the National Trust, is worth the ascent for the 360 degree view – north to London and south to the channel; quite spectacular. You continue on along a good track through woodland and join the Greensands Way as you make your way to Holmbury St. Mary, your last village for some nine miles. Although not quite halfway it has a fine inn!

WALKING INSTRUCTIONS – Reaching the road in Coldharbour with The Plough Inn opposite; do not cross the road but turn right onto the ascending track, signed – Leith Hill and Cricket Club. The ascending track bears left and soon reach the Coldharbour Cricket Club field on the right – the highest cricket club in the south-east! Gaining the parking area and entrance to the National Trust property. Keep to the left-hand path/track and keep straight ahead along it ignoring all other paths. In about 12 mins the Greensands Way comes in from the right. Bear left and ascend the short steep wide path that leads directly to the tower on Leith Hill; absorb the panorama!

Leaving the tower keep to the left-hand track near the hill's edge at first and slowly descend. The path signs have the initials GW (Greensands Way) in the middle. Ignore all other paths and keep ahead and in more than ½ mile (about 14 mins) gain Leith Hill Lane. Turn right and left to follow the Greensands Way. Continue in woodland and take the second track on the right, still on Greensands Way which you follow all the way to Holmbury St. Mary. Continue along the public bridleway and in ¼ mile turn left and continue on the track through woodland of Great Foxmore Wood. Later the track becomes a path before reverting back to a track as you walk through Pasture Wood. Some 20 mins from Leith Hill Road reach Pasture Wood Road. Turn left and soon gain Horsham Road, with the King's Head Inn and Pitland Street ahead on the southern edge of Holmbury St. Mary. Cross into Pitland Street for the next hilly section! Bus stop on the right for Dorking.

I had taken 21,011 steps to get here, burning off 706 calories!

Coldharbour Cricket Club Ground.

LEITH HILL – The 18th. Century Gothic tower stands *19.5* m *(64* ft.) *tall and from the top just over the* 1,000 *foot a.s.l.* (305m), *is the highest point in S.E. England. The indicator on the top, from which some* 13 *counties can be seen, is in memory of Walker Miles and a key player in the creation of the Ramblers Association. Leith Hill Place below was inherited by the composer Ralph Vaughan Williams, who in* 1944 *gave it to the National Trust. There are several members of his family buried in Wotton churchyard, on the right of the steps at the back.*
www.nationaltrust.org.uk/leith-hill

HOLMBURY ST. MARY – *Holmbury Hill, nearby is* 261m *(857* ft.) *the fourth highest point in Surrey. The church dedicated to St. Mary was built in* 1879. *Beyond the northern edge of the village is Holmbury YHA, the first purpose built youth hostel.*

Leith Hill view.

Greensands Way logo signs, showing the tower on Leith Hill.

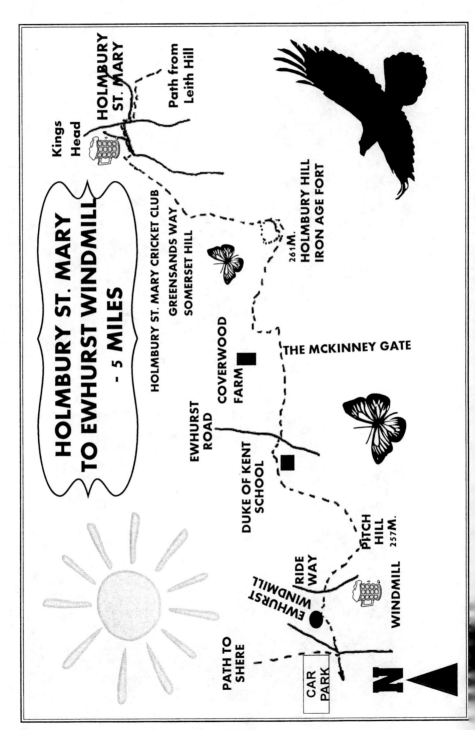

HOLMBURY ST. MARY to EWHURST WINDMILL
– 5 MILES
– allow 2 hours.

Maps – OS 1:25,000 **Explorer Series Nos.**
- 146 – **Dorking, Box Hill & Reigate.**
- 145 – **Guildford & Farnham**

Inns – Kings Head, Holmbury St. Mary. ¼ mile from route down Ride Way is the Windmill Inn.

ABOUT THE SECTION – You soon return to the hills, first to Holmbury Hill – 261m., a fine vantage point and the remains of an Iron Age fort. Still following the Greensand Way, you continue onto The Huntwood Car Park and cross open undulating country to Ewhurst Road and the Duke of Kent School. When I reached here a full scale replica of a Spitfire was on display. Pressing on past the school you ascend to Pitch Hill – 257m. Descending to Ride Way and Pitch Hill Car park you soon reach Ewhurst Windmill. Soon after you gain Horseblock Hollow Car Park, where you leave the hills and Greensand Way to head northwards to Shere through woodland – your next section.

WALKING INSTRUCTIONS – Cross Horsham Road (B2126) – bus stop on the right for Dorking. Cross to the right to Pitland Street and turn left up it, passing a historical plaque on Lyngate House on the left to Victor E. Yarsley OBE BsC - 1901 - 1994 - Plastics pioneer. Follow the lane left soon passing the King's Head Inn to the right. Where is curves left turn right onto a track signposted – Holmbury Cricket Club. At the top turn left, still on a track and pass the cricket ground on the right – you are still and will be on all this section, on the signed Greensand Way. ¼ mile later reach a path junction, two pine trees and a metal seat on Somerset Hill; turn left onto another track. The path soon forks and keep right as the path now undulates through silver birch along the escarpment edge to Holmbury Iron Age Fort on the right to an extensive vantage point over this part of south-eastern England.

Bear right along the fort's edge, passing a historical information board and bear left, past the triangulation pillar, now on a track. As advised by path sign – footpath only – keep left and descend to The Huntwood

Fenced path path near Coverwood Farm.

Car park, turning right and left to gain Radnor Road. Cross and keep ahead for a few meters before turning left on a track. Shortly after turn right, as path signed, and walk along a fenced path to The Kckinney Gate (marked) with Coverwood Farm well to your right. You are now away from the trees and passing open fields, with cattle and sheep, as you keep straight ahead ascending and then descending to Ewhurst Road ½ mile away.

Cross onto the drive of the Duke of Kent School. Initially, walk up the drive, but as signed keep right onto an ascending path. Follow the path upwards in woodland, bearing left and right to a kissing gate. Continue on the path leftwards to steps to a track junction. Keep left now on a level track and pass small fields and a house on the right. At the end of the house garden turn right and ascend to another path junction. Keep left and now level walking. Again take the "footpath only" path on the left and soon reach the "summit" of Pitch Hill" - 257m and its two triangulation pillars. Pass them and bear right onto a wide path/track in silver birch, soon descending to Pitch Hill Car Park and road – Ride Way.

Cross and continue on a track past Mill Cottage and into Shere Manor Estate, to Four Winds. Keep left and pass Ewhurst Windmill as the track becomes a path descending to a road with Horseblock Hollow Car park on the left. Here you leave the Greensand Way and turn right onto a bridleway and the start of the wooded section to Shere.

View from Holmbury Hill.

HOLMBURY HILL – *261m* – *857* **feet and fourth highest point in Surrey. There is a cairn with direction finder. The Iron Age fort dates from the 1st. Century AD and has a double ditches and was excavated in** *1929* **by S. E. Winbolt. The area is a popular mountain bike route; hence the footpath only paths!**

DUKE OF KENT SCHOOL – **Founded in** *1976* **by the Royal Air Force Benevolent Fund and named after Prince George, the Duke of Kent** *1902-1942,* **who died in a air crash. The pupils at first. were mostly the sons of former and serving RAF personnel. In** *1978* **the school became co-educational. The house** – **Woolpit House, was built by Sir Henry Doulton of pottery fame in** *1886.*

Spitfire and Duke of Kent School.

PITCH HILL – 257m – Another stunning vantage point over the Weald and South Downs.

EWHURST WINDMILL – Grade 2 listed building dating back to the 19th. Century. The circular tower has four floors. Aptly, just down the main road - Ride Way - is The Windmill Inn.

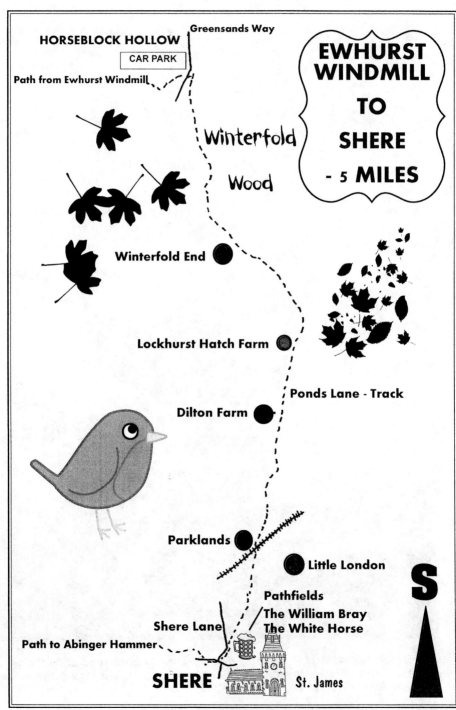

EWHURST WINDMILL TO SHERE
– 5 MILES
– allow 2 hours.

Map – OS 1:25,000 **Explorer Series No.** 146 – **Dorking, Box Hill & Reigate.**

Inns – The William Bray, The White Horse; Shere.

Tearoom - Shere.

ABOUT THE SECTION – You now head northwards............gently downhill. First through a magnificent wooded valley and then along a track and lane to Shere, which is regarded as the prettiest village in Surrey. It is a delight with many amenities, a river, interesting houses and a church dedicated to St. James. Aptly, as he is the patron saint of Pilgrims to Santiago de Compostella, as Shere is on the medieval pilgrims route from Winchester to Canterbury. In the church you can get your pilgrims passport stamped. The route is quiet, and perhaps a mountain biker or two, you have the area to yourself.

WALKING INSTRUCTIONS – **Opposite Horseblock Hollow car park,** turn right, as bridle-path signed onto a path into Winterfold Wood. The path soon becomes a track as you gently descend – you will descend from 235m. To Shere at approximately 90m – so some 500 feet, although you will hardly notice you are descending. First you walk through a delightful pine valley and in little over ½ mile – approx 12 mins – you cross a minor road. Keep ahead and pass a pond on your left and reach a gate. Turn left through it and continue in woodland along a wide path for another ½ mile. A path on the right joins yours, but just keep left now along a stony path. In ½ mile pass a house on the left and keep ahead now on a track/drive. Soon keep right, as bridle-path signed, along a path leading to a lane (track) with Lockhurst Hatch Farm on the right.

Pine tree valley at the start of this section.

Keep ahead along the track – Ponds Lane – and soon pass Cherrymans on the left. Keep straight ahead and soon along a Public Byway. Pass the turning for Dilton Farm on the right, and keep ahead along the lane/track. This curves right and left and passes Ponds Farm on the left, before reaching houses of Parklands on the right. Immediately after turn left and cross the railway line, with care. Having reached the other-side turn right onto a defined path through woodland. Cross a minor road from Little London to your left, and keep ahead on the path to a path junction. Turn right then left onto a bridleway (Dark Lane), and almost immediately, right as bridle-path signed. Follow this to the houses of Shere, soon walking along Pathfields to reach Shere Lane. Turn left and pass The William Bray and White Horse Inns and shops and turn right to St. James church.

SHERE – The River Tillingbourne flows through; as it does in Abinger Hammer. The unspoilt village has shops, tearoom, a museum, and two inns. There are 34 listed buildings built before 1830 and the village centre is a conservation area. Several films have been shot here including scenes from Bridget Jones.

St. James church - was built in 1190 in Early English style – pointed arches. The South Porch has a late Norman archway. The font is dated 1200 and the oak Crusader Chest dates from this time. In the Chancel is the window of an anchoress cell in the north wall, built in 1329. The anchoress – Christine Carpenter – could see the altar and could receive bread and wine. There are several 15th. And 16th century brasses and many tombs to the Bray family in the Bray Chapel – Lords of the Manor of Shere. The St. Nicholas Chapel built between 1370-1390 has a window commemorating the end of the War of the Roses.

Shere village from outside the church.

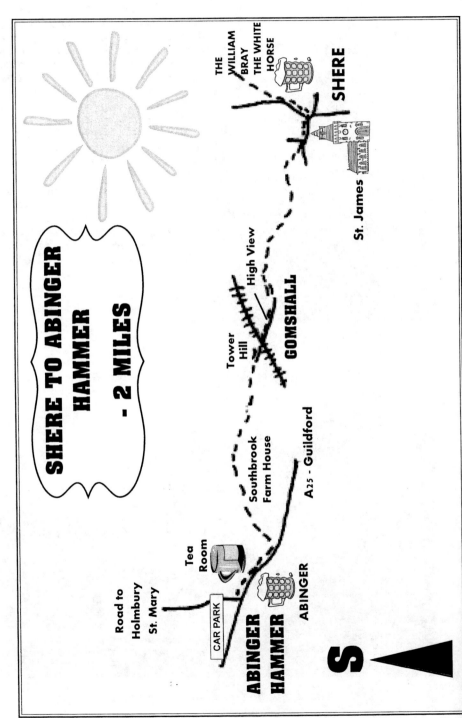

SHERE to ABINGER HAMMER
– 2 MILES
– allow 1 hours.

Map – OS 1:25,000 Explorer Series No. 146 – Dorking, Box Hill & Reigate.

Inn – Abinger, Abinger Hammer.

Tearoom - Abinger Hammer.

ABOUT THE SECTION – The final couple of miles on good paths. You skirt the village of Gomshall which has a railway station, but the trains are every two hours! There are several inns and restaurants there. Reaching Abinger Hammer you have several options for your return home – by bus or car. Thus completing a surprising "hilly" circuit in south-eastern England.

WALKING INSTRUCTIONS – Continue past St. James church to the first road on the right. Here on the other-side on the right is a gate and footpath sign. Follow the defined path to a path T junction and turn left – this is part of Cycle Route No. 22 which you first met as you left Abinger Hammer, a few hours ago! Keep the hedge on your left. The path soon turns right then left to the houses of Gomshall. Reaching a junction at the houses turn left, still on Cycle Route 22, as you walk along Gravel Pits Lane – a track. Reaching a road – High View - keep straight ahead along it to the railway line. Turn right to pass under it at Tower Hill – interesting house here, and immediately left onto a bridleway and still part of Cycleway No. 22.

Continue on the path which soon bears right and becomes a drive to the houses of Wonham Way. Keep left and then right to follow the concrete drive, crossing a stream and passing Southbrook Farm House on the left. Keep ahead to the A25 and the Hunters Moon Farm opposite. Turn right back into Abinger Hammer with the Abinger Inn on the left. Just after is Hackhurst Lane - you walked up at the start. A little further along the road is the Tea Room, bus stop (Dorking/Guildford), and close to the start of the road to Holmbury St. Mary, on the left is the small village car park.

Congratulations on completing the walk!

House at Tower Hill, immediately before the railway bridge.

The tranquil River Tillingbourne in Abinger Hammer.

FOLLOW THE COUNTRY CODE

* Be safe - plan ahead and follow any signs.

* Leave gates and property as you find them.

* Protect plants and animals, and take your litter home.

* Keep dogs under close control.

* Consider other people.

* Take only photographs, leave only footprints.

WALK LOG

PLACE	MILE NO	TIME/COMMENTS
Abinger Hammer	0	
Wotton	3	
Coldharbour	7	
Leith Hill - 292m.	8	
Holmbury St. Mary	11	
Holmbury Hill - 261m	12 1/2	
Pitch Hill - 257m,	15	
Ewhurst Windmill	15 1/2	
Winterfold Wood	16	
Ponds Lane	18	
Shere	21	
Abinger Hammer	23	

Weather ....

Birds seen ....

....

....

Complete this walk and get a special Embroidered badge and signed certificate.

Date of walk .... Time taken ....

Name
....

Address
....

....

Badge and certificate - £7.00 each including post and packing.

Send form to - The John Merrill Foundation,
32, Holmesdale, Waltham Cross, Hertfordshire. EN8 8QY

Order on line - www.johnmerrillwalkguides.co.uk

OTHER BOOKS BY REVD. JOHN N. MERRILL

CIRCULAR WALK GUIDES –
SHORT CIRCULAR WALKS IN THE PEAK DISTRICT – Vol. 1,2, 3 and 9
CIRCULAR WALKS IN WESTERN PEAKLAND
SHORT CIRCULAR WALKS IN THE STAFFORDSHIRE MOORLANDS
SHORT CIRCULAR WALKS – TOWNS & VILLAGES OF THE PEAK DISTRICT
SHORT CIRCULAR WALKS AROUND MATLOCK
SHORT CIRCULAR WALKS IN "PEAK PRACTICE COUNTRY."
SHORT CIRCULAR WALKS IN THE DUKERIES
SHORT CIRCULAR WALKS IN SOUTH YORKSHIRE
SHORT CIRCULAR WALKS IN SOUTH DERBYSHIRE
SHORT CIRCULAR WALKS AROUND BUXTON
SHORT CIRCULAR WALKS AROUND WIRKSWORTH
SHORT CIRCULAR WALKS IN THE HOPE VALLEY
40 SHORT CIRCULAR WALKS IN THE PEAK DISTRICT
CIRCULAR WALKS ON KINDER & BLEAKLOW
SHORT CIRCULAR WALKS IN SOUTH NOTTINGHAMSHIRE
SHORT CIRCULAR WALKS IN CHESHIRE
SHORT CIRCULAR WALKS IN WEST YORKSHIRE
WHITE PEAK DISTRICT AIRCRAFT WRECKS
CIRCULAR WALKS IN THE DERBYSHIRE DALES
SHORT CIRCULAR WALKS FROM BAKEWELL
SHORT CIRCULAR WALKS IN LATHKILL DALE
CIRCULAR WALKS IN THE WHITE PEAK
SHORT CIRCULAR WALKS IN EAST DEVON
SHORT CIRCULAR WALKS AROUND HARROGATE
SHORT CIRCULAR WALKS IN CHARNWOOD FOREST
SHORT CIRCULAR WALKS AROUND CHESTERFIELD
SHORT CIRCULAR WALKS IN THE YORKS DALES – Vol 1 – Southern area.
SHORT CIRCULAR WALKS IN THE AMBER VALLEY (Derbyshire)
SHORT CIRCULAR WALKS IN THE LAKE DISTRICT
SHORT CIRCULAR WALKS IN THE NORTH YORKSHIRE MOORS
SHORT CIRCULAR WALKS IN EAST STAFFORDSHIRE
LONG CIRCULAR WALKS IN THE PEAK DISTRICT – Vol.1, 2, 3, 4 and 5.
DARK PEAK AIRCRAFT WRECK WALKS
LONG CIRCULAR WALKS IN THE STAFFORDSHIRE MOORLANDS
LONG CIRCULAR WALKS IN CHESHIRE
WALKING THE TISSINGTON TRAIL
WALKING THE HIGH PEAK TRAIL
WALKING THE MONSAL TRAIL & SETT VALLEY TRAILS
PEAK DISTRICT WALKING – TEN "TEN MILER'S" – Vol One and Two
CLIMB THE PEAKS OF THE PEAK DISTRICT
PEAK DISTRICT WALK A MONTH Vols One,Two, Three, Four, Five & Six
TRAIN TO WALK Vol. One – The Hope Valley Line
DERBYSHIRE LOST VILLAGE WALKS –Vol One and Two.
CIRCULAR WALKS IN DOVEDALE AND THE MANIFOLD VALLEY
CIRCULAR WALKS AROUND GLOSSOP
WALKING THE LONGDENDALE TRAIL
WALKING THE UPPER DON TRAIL
SHORT CIRCULAR WALKS IN CANNOCK CHASE
CIRCULAR WALKS IN THE DERWENT VALLEY
WALKING THE TRAILS OF NORTH-EAST DERBYSHIRE
WALKING THE PENNINE BRIDLEWAY & CIRCULAR WALKS
SHORT CIRCULAR WALKS ON THE NEW RIVER & SOUTH-EAST HERTFORDSHIRE
SHORT CIRCULAR WALKS IN EPPING FOREST
WALKING THE STREETS OF LONDON
LONG CIRCULAR WALKS IN EASTERN HERTFORDSHIRE
LONG CIRCULAR WALKS IN WESTERN HERTFORDSHIRE
WALKS IN THE LONDON BOROUGH OF ENFIELD
WALKS IN THE LONDON BOROUGH OF BARNET
WALKS IN THE LONDON BOROUGH OF HARINGEY
WALK IN THE LONDON BOROUGH OF WALTHAM FOREST
SHORT CIRCULAR WALKS AROUND HERTFORD
THE BIG WALKS OF LONDON
SHORT CIRCULAR WALKS AROUND BISHOP'S STORTFORD
SHORT CIRCULAR WALKS AROUND EPPING DISTRICT
CIRCULAR WALKS IN THE BOROUGH OF BROXBOURNE
LONDON INTERFAITH WALKS – Vol 1 and Vol. 2
LONG CIRCULAR WALKS IN THE NORTH CHILTERNS
SHORT CIRCULAR WALKS IN EASTERN HERTFORDSHIRE
WORCESTERSHIRE VILLAGE WALKS by Des Wright
WARWICKSHIRE VILLAGE WALKS by Des Wright
WALKING AROUND THE ROYAL PARKS OF LONDON
WALKS IN THE LONDON BOROUGH OF CHELSEA AND ROYAL KENSINGTON

CANAL WALKS –
VOL 1 – DERBYSHIRE & NOTTINGHAMSHIRE
VOL 2 – CHESHIRE & STAFFORDSHIRE
VOL 3 – STAFFORDSHIRE
VOL 4 – THE CHESHIRE RING
VOL 5 – THE GRANTHAM CANAL
VOL 6 – SOUTH YORKSHIRE
VOL 7 – THE TRENT & MERSEY CANAL
VOL 8 – WALKING THE DERBY CANAL RING
VOL 9 – WALKING THE LLANGOLLEN CANAL
VOL 10 – CIRCULAR WALKS ON THE CHESTERFIELD CANAL
VOL 11 – CIRCULAR WALKS ON THE CROMFORD CANAL
Vol.13 – SHORT CIRCULAR WALKS ON THE RIVER LEE NAVIGATION –Vol. 1 – North
Vol. 14 – SHORT CIRCULAR WALKS ON THE RIVER STORT NAVIGATION
Vol.15 – SHORT CIRCULAR WALKS ON THE RIVER LEE NAVIGATION – Vol. 2 – South
Vol. 16 – WALKING THE CANALS OF LONDON
Vol. 17 – WALKING THE RIVER LEE NAVIGATION
Vol. 20 – SHORT CIRCULAR WALKS IN THE COLNE VALLEY
Vol 21 – THE BLACKWATER & CHELMER NAVIGATION – End to End.
Vol. 22 – NOTTINGHAM'S LOST CANAL by Bernard Chell.
Vol. 23 – WALKING THE RIVER WEY & GODALMING NAVIGATIONS END TO END
Vol25 – WALKING THE GRAND UNION CANAL – LONDON TO BIRMINGHAM.

JOHN MERRILL DAY CHALLENGE WALKS
WHITE PEAK CHALLENGE WALK
THE HAPPY HIKER – WHITE PEAK – CHALLENGE WALK No.2
DARK PEAK CHALLENGE WALK
PEAK DISTRICT END TO END WALKS
STAFFORDSHIRE MOORLANDS CHALLENGE WALK
THE LITTLE JOHN CHALLENGE WALK
YORKSHIRE DALES CHALLENGE WALK
NORTH YORKSHIRE MOORS CHALLENGE WALK
LAKELAND CHALLENGE WALK
THE RUTLAND WATER CHALLENGE WALK
MALVERN HILLS CHALLENGE WALK
THE SALTER'S WAY

THE SNOWDON CHALLENGE
CHARNWOOD FOREST CHALLENGE WALK
THREE COUNTIES CHALLENGE WALK (Peak District).
CAL-DER-WENT WALK
THE QUANTOCK WAY
BELVOIR WITCHES CHALLENGE WALK
THE CARNEDDAU CHALLENGE WALK
THE SWEET PEA CHALLENGE WALK
THE LINCOLNSHIRE WOLDS – BLACK DEATH – CHALLENGE WALK
JENNIFER'S CHALLENGE WALK
THE EPPING FOREST CHALLENGE WALK
THE THREE BOROUGH CHALLENGE WALK – NORTH LONDON
THE HERTFORD CHALLENGE WALK

INSTRUCTION & RECORD –
HIKE TO BE FIT....STROLLING WITH JOHN
THE JOHN MERRILL WALK RECORD BOOK
HIKE THE WORLD – John Merrill's guide to walking & Backpacking.

MULTIPLE DAY WALKS –
THE RIVERS'S WAY
PEAK DISTRICT: HIGH LEVEL ROUTE
PEAK DISTRICT MARATHONS
THE LIMEY WAY
THE PEAKLAND WAY
COMPO'S WAY by Alan Hiley
THE BRIGHTON WAY

THE PILGRIM WALKS SERIES –
THE WALSINGHAM WAY – Ely to Walsingham – 72 miles
THE WALSINGHAM WAY – Kings Lynn to Walsingham – 35 miles
THE WALSINGHAM WAY – Bury St. Edmunds to Walsingham – 77 miles
TURN LEFT AT GRANJA DE LA MORERUELA – 700 miles
NORTH TO SANTIAGO DE COMPOSTELA, VIA FATIMA – 650 miles
St. OLAV'S WAY – Oslo to Trondheim – 400 miles
St. WINEFRIDE'S WAY – St. Asaph to Holywell
St. ALBANS WAY – Waltham Abbey to St. Albans – 26 miles
St. KENELM TRAIL by John Price – Clent Hills to Winchcombe – 60 miles
DERBYSHIRE PILGRIMAGES
LONDON TO CANTERBURY – 75 MILES
LONDON TO ST. ALBANS – 36 MILES
LONDON TO WALSINGHAM – 194 MILES
FOLKESTONE, HYTHE TO CANTERBURY – 25 MILES
THE JOHN SCHORNE PEREGRINATIONS – 27 MILES by M. Mooney
ST CEDD'S PILGRIMAGE WALK – 24 miles
ST BIRINIUS PILGRIMAGE WALK – 26 miles
OUR LADY OF ULTING PILGRIMAGE WALK – 16 MILES
OUR LADY OF CAVERSHAM PILGRIMAGE WALK – 38 Miles
THE MANDEVILLE MONKS WAY – 32 MILES
THE ESSEX PRIORIES WAY – 26 MILES
walking the cammino di assisi – 320 km.
A FUNERAL CELEBRANT'S DIARY
THE AYLESFORD PILGRIMAGE
THREE SOUTH-EAST OUR LADY PILGRIMAGE WALKS.
MY STORY OF WALKING THE BON HOMMES WAY

COAST WALKS & NATIONAL TRAILS –
ISLE OF WIGHT COAST PATH
PEMBROKESHIRE COAST PATH
THE CLEVELAND WAY
WALKING ANGELSEY'S COASTLINE.
WALKING THE COASTLINE OF THE CHANNEL ISLANDS
THE ISLE OF MAN COASTAL PATH – "The Way of the Gull."
A WALK AROUND HAYLING ISLAND
A WALK AROUND THE ISLE OF SHEPPEY
A WALK AROUND THE ISLE OF JERSEY
WALKING AROUND THE ISLANDS OF ESSEX

DERBYSHIRE & PEAK DISTRICT HISTORICAL GUIDES –
A to Z GUIDE OF THE PEAK DISTRICT
DERBYSHIRE INNS – an A to Z guide
HALLS AND CASTLES OF THE PEAK DISTRICT & DERBYSHIRE
TOURING THE PEAK DISTRICT & DERBYSHIRE BY CAR
DERBYSHIRE FOLKLORE
PUNISHMENT IN DERBYSHIRE
CUSTOMS OF THE PEAK DISTRICT & DERBYSHIRE
WINSTER – a souvenir guide
ARKWRIGHT OF CROMFORD
LEGENDS OF DERBYSHIRE
DERBYSHIRE FACTS & RECORDS
TALES FROM THE MINES by Geoffrey Carr
PEAK DISTRICT PLACE NAMES by Martin Spray
DERBYSHIRE THROUGH THE AGES – Vol 1 –DERBYSHIRE IN PREHISTORIC TIMES
SIR JOSEPH PAXTON
FLORENCE NIGHTINGALE
JOHN SMEDLEY
BONNIE PRINCE CHARLIE & 20 mile walk.
THE STORY OF THE EARLS AND DUKES OF DEVONSHIRE

JOHN MERRILL'S MAJOR WALKS –
TURN RIGHT AT LAND'S END
WITH MUSTARD ON MY BACK
TURN RIGHT AT DEATH VALLEY
EMERALD COAST WALK
I CHOSE TO WALK – Why I walk etc.
A WALK IN OHIO – 1,310 miles around the Buckeye Trail.
I AM GUIDED – the story of John's life.
SKETCH BOOKS –
SKETCHES OF THE PEAK DISTRICT
COLOUR BOOK:–
THE PEAK DISTRICT........something to remember her by.
OVERSEAS GUIDES –
HIKING IN NEW MEXICO – Vol I – The Sandia and Manzano Mountains.
Vol 2 – Hiking "Billy the Kid" Country.
Vol 4 – N.W. area – "Hiking Indian Country."
"WALKING IN DRACULA COUNTRY" – Romania.
WALKING THE TRAILS OF THE HONG KONG ISLANDS.

VISITOR GUIDES – MATLOCK. BAKEWELL. ASHBOURNE.

By being in the countryside you reconnect with nature and your true self. It is just you and your two feet along the path through a varied landscape of fields, woods, hills and mountains. Passing flowing streams and rivers and being close to nature. The birds watch your pass, and hop infront of you along the trees branches. Squirrels run to the nearest tree and watch from above as you pass. Butterflies flit from flower to flower, while the countryside flowers rear their heads seeking the warmth of the summer sun. Hawks circle above looking for food and woodpeckers shriek and fly to another tree to peck. The seasons bring different sights and sounds. Winter all is quiet but as spring begins to enfold the birds are busy nesting and the leaves begin to uncurl. Early summer brings deep vibrant colours enrched by rain. But as the endless cycle of life constantly turns, they begin to fade and turn for a few days a golden hue as a final fling before hibernating in winter preparing to begin the cycle again.

Revd. John N. Merrill - December 2019.

**Revd. John N. Merrill
HonMuniv
Funeral Celebrant,
Weddings, Ashes
Internment,
Sermons, Talks &
Pilgrimages.
Multi-Faith Minister**
"Embracing and honouring
all faiths and none."

John has been following his own unique spiritual path all his life and is guided and looked after. He was brought up a Christian and confirmed at the age of 11. He went to a Quaker Boarding school for five years and developed his love of the countryside and outdoors. He became fascinated with Tibet and whilst retaining his Christian roots, became immersed in Buddhism, later spending four years at the Tara Buddhist Centre in Derbyshire. He now incorporates Taoism and attends the Chinese Buddhist Centre in London. With his thirst for knowledge and discovery he paid attention to other faiths and appreciated their teachings and values. Late in life he decided it was time to reveal his spiritual beliefs and practices and discovered the Interfaith Seminary.

Here for two years he learnt in more depth the whole spectrum of faiths, including Jainism, Paganism, Mother Earth, Buddhism, Hinduism, Islam, Judaism, Sikhism, Celtic Worship and Shamanism. This is an ongoing exploration without end. All faiths have their own beauty and path. All lead to the same destination. He was ordained on July 17th, 2010 as an multi-faith Minister and Spiritual Counsellor. He has now done more than 500 funeral services and numerous weddings, including one in Sarajevo, Bosnia.

"May you go in peace, with joy in your heart
and may the divine be always at your side."

THE JOHN MERRILL MINISTRY, Enfield, London. EN8 8QY
Email - universalmonk@outlook.com
Tel. 01992 762776